DIESES BUCH GEHÖRT:

I0394102

www.ingramcontent.com/pod-product-compliance
Lightning Source LLC
Chambersburg PA
CBHW021844170526
45157CB00007B/2938
9781074783341